Chocolate
make and mould
your own chocolate bars

Utensils

chocolate bar mould
[not to be put in the oven or in a dishwasher]

flexible spatula

long straight spoon

bain-marie pan

zester

cooking thermometer

Chocolate
make and mould
your own chocolate bars

Anne Deblois

photography by Jean-Pierre Duval

With help from Laurence Alemanno
and Jean-René Jahény

WAVERLEY
BOOKS

Contents

Chocolate, a right royal story

By Jean-René Jahéry

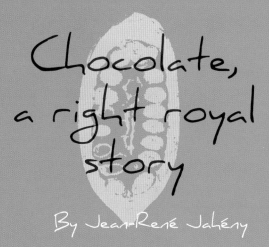

The great Cardinal Richelieu used to drink multiple cups of chocolate in an attempt to relieve the pain in his spleen. And in spite of that, he went about haughty and alone, with his natural hypochondria and bouts of deep depression. Did he suffer from magnesium deficiency? Were his chocolate rations sufficient? Who knows?

Louis XIV, who had learned a lot from his mother Anne of Austria, was not above preparing his own little chocolate snack with numerous bain-maries and egg yolks according to a very personal recipe. He would disappear into the small apartments behind the ceremonial rooms at Versailles, to satisfy his natural penchant.

The Sun King's young wife, Maria Theresa of Austria, who, in spite of her name, was Spanish (she was the daughter of Philip IV of Spain), when she married the young king at Saint-Jean-de-Luz, turned him into a chocolate "addict". As she crossed the Bidassoa once and for all she took with her in her luggage all she needed to prepare the delicious beverage. Did she suspect she would never again cross the Pyrenees? No doubt she did, and it did come to pass. But, as far as chocolate was concerned, she had taken precautions.

The Spanish had been familiar with the use of chocolate for over a century, but only the Spanish court knew how to use it and savour it and held the secret of how to prepare it. It was the "food of the gods" as the Maya said, for the sole pleasure of kings.

Young woman drinking chocolate,
by François de Troy (1645-1730), oil on canvas,
25 x 34 cm, exhibited in Berlin (Germany),
Gemäldegalerie

In 1502 Christopher Columbus had, of course, been aware of the existence of these famous pods but he had not guessed how important they were. Yet they were being used as trading currency. It was Hernan Cortez who, in 1519 while eating with the Aztec emperor Montezuma before finally bumping him off, discovered the importance of this beverage. He rapidly appreciated not only its taste but also its nourishing, strengthening and of course aphrodisiac qualities. Otherwise, what would be the point? Why bother?

However, at the time chocolate, called "cacahualt" by the Maya, was only taken as a bitter drink, sweetened with honey only at the Spanish court. The Maya mixed it with water and spices and made a widely enjoyed restorative drink. Only in the nineteenth century was chocolate invented in powder form, and later as bars of chocolate. We will return to this later.

The cacao tree is easy to grow. Native to the Orinoco basin, it is a plant which grows "under cover", ie under the protection of taller trees that provide shade. It needs water and heat. Along its branches and trunk grow big fruits, 20-cm long, that are commonly called pods.

But it is no easy task to prepare chocolate. It was a craft until the nineteenth century and it was Fry's hydraulic press in Bristol in 1728 then, above all, Pelletier's in 1770, that brought chocolate into the age of mass consumption.

Maria Theresa, albeit queen of France, was obliged to use the same methods as the American Indians: once the beans had been extracted from the pods, between 40 to 50 in a pod, they were left to ferment for about four days, then put in the open air to dry. Finally the kernels were roasted on a heated stone. This was a delicate business because the cocoa had to acquire a good colour and flavour without being spoiled. The kernels or nibs were then ground to collect the cocoa powder and extract the cocoa butter. Later, this butter was to be widely used in the cosmetic and pharmaceutical industries. All that Maria Theresa now had to do was to prepare the divine powder with mainly water – at least until the mid-nineteenth century.

The Europeans mechanised the manufacturing process and as of 1820 production really took off. It was the Swiss in the nineteenth century who finally added milk. Then the English, the Belgians and the French who were for a long time the leading producers, with such famous brands and inventors as Meunier and Poulain, refined the recipes by adding all that makes for the subtlety of contemporary chocolates: hazelnuts, orange, fruit, walnuts, etc.

We must be careful not to forget such famous names as the Swiss Suchard, Kohler, Tobler and Lindt, and the Dutch Van Houten without whom chocolate cakes would not be what they are!

A particular tribute must be paid to the Swiss Cailler who was the first in 1819 to produce a bar of chocolate. He had just invented plain dark chocolate. This is a discovery of very great interest to us in a book which aims solely to reveal chocolate recipes!

Centuries later, the agrology of cocoa has changed a lot. The numerous species from the rustic Forestero, the Griollo to the Trinitario, have gradually given way to the one which Linné in 1737 was already calling "Theobroma", the "food of the gods". And the geography of the cacao tree has undergone profound change. It crossed the Atlantic and became acclimatised in Africa. So the European producers supplied their colonies with an export crop with a high added value. They could become owners of their own plantations and in the end made great savings in transport.

Today the situation has evolved as independent African states have taken over, or at least so we must hope. The four leading African countries for cocoa production are Ivory Coast with 34%, Ghana with 18%, followed by Nigeria and Cameroon. Also we must not neglect the American production and pods from the Philippines and Java.

Once the drink of princes, emperors and kings, chocolate has become a universal treat. We have difficulty imagining that it was possible to live without a bar of chocolate for a snack and a big bowl of cocoa to warm us on a cold day. And shame on the memory of Anne of Austria and Maria Theresa who viewed their chocolate as being as precious as Inca gold and selfishly kept this delicacy secret from their subjects. We will be more lenient with Louis XIV who prepared it all by himself. Let us now embark boldly on all these recipes with chocolate in bars and squares which will make us all healthy, and will make women, without a doubt ... deliciously beautiful!

Technical matters

By Anne Deblois

◉ How to melt the chocolate

The best way to melt chocolate, whether dark, milk or white, is using a bain-marie or double-boiler. This technique consists of placing the container holding the chocolate in another pan of hot water. In this way, the heat is gentle and constant. The chocolate thus melts slowly, and gradually acquires a smooth, homogeneous texture. There are shops that sell bain-marie pans, where the two pans (one for the water, the other for the chocolate) are joined together in one piece. These are ideal for making the chocolate bar recipes in this book: all you have to do is pour water (up to about half-way) into the lower part of the pan and put it on the heat.

We also recommend you use a flexible spatula to stir and work the chocolate.

To make your chocolate bars two techniques are suggested:

1. Fast and easy

The first technique is fast and easy; all you have to do is melt the chocolate in the bain-marie until it is liquid and smooth, then add the various ingredients, following the steps described in the recipes.

In this way you will get smooth, shiny bars, but the drawback will be that they melt quickly in the hand. You will probably need to keep them in the refrigerator and this may slightly alter the taste of the chocolate.

2. Tempering

To obtain harder, shinier bars, the second technique proposed is tempering the chocolate. Tempering is a technique that makes the chocolate follow a very precise temperature curve so that the cocoa butter crystallises and stabilises.

dark : 50/55 °C
milk : 45/50 °C

bain-marie

big container

a few seconds in the
bain-marie

dark : 30/32 °C
milk : 29/30 °C

room
temperature

dark : 27/29 °C
milk : 26/28 °C

The temperatures for dark chocolate and milk chocolate and the steps to follow are given below:

◎ Method

Break your chocolate up into rough pieces. Put them in the bain-marie. Heat on a very low flame, making sure the water only simmers (does not boil).

As soon as the chocolate begins to melt, stir constantly with the flexible spatula to keep the temperature uniform. Check the temperature with a cooking or sugar thermometer and let the chocolate heat until it reaches a temperature between 50 and 55 °C (45 to 50 °C for milk chocolate).

Pour the chocolate into a large container. Stir the chocolate, spreading it out then bringing the edges back to the centre to keep the consistency uniform with none of it hardening around the edges. Keep doing this until the chocolate reaches a temperature of 27 to 29 °C (26 to 28 °C for milk chocolate).

Pour the chocolate back into the bain-marie, and heat on a very low flame, stirring to obtain a chocolate mixture that is between 30 and 32 °C. Be careful, this step is very fast. It takes only a few seconds for the chocolate to reach this temperature.

◎ Moulding and setting the chocolate, and removing the chocolate from the mould

1. Moulding

Put your chocolate bar mould on a flat surface.

When your chocolate has reached the desired temperature, pour it into the mould, scraping the pan with the flexible spatula.

(If you use a bain-marie pan, make sure you pour the chocolate from the side opposite the opening for the water.)

To smooth off your preparation, leave the mould sitting flat on the worktop. With little jerks, slide it horizontally from back to front so that the chocolate spreads out over the mould and has a smooth surface.

2. Setting

Leave your preparation for at least 3 hours in the refrigerator before removing it from the mould. Thereafter, non-tempered chocolate should be kept preferably in the refrigerator wrapped in some aluminium foil. Tempered chocolate can be kept in a cool, dry place, or in the refrigerator depending on the texture desired.

3. Removing the chocolate bar from the mould

When you take the mould out of the refrigerator twist two opposing corners (eg top left and bottom right), then the other two corners so that the chocolate comes unstuck from the mould. You should then see the bar lifting when you bend the mould. Place your hand over the bar of chocolate, then turn the mould over in order to catch the chocolate. If you use a three-bar mould, you must be careful to gently hold the three bars in place before tipping the mould over to avoid breaking them.

If the bars do not come unstuck when you twist the mould, run the bottom of the mould for just a few seconds under very hot water. You could also run the point of a knife-blade round the bar to detach the edges.

◎ What chocolate to use

The range of chocolates you can use to create your own bars is as vast as the varieties of chocolate that exist. The chocolate indicated for each recipe is only a suggestion and can easily be replaced by your own choice of chocolate, depending on the taste that you are looking for.

Your basic raw material is the chocolate, whether in the form of bars, blocks or pistoles (big chocolate chips).

For common chocolate you can get supplies from supermarkets where you will find classic bars of chocolate or so-called "cooking" chocolate, or from an industrial chocolatier if you want to use pistoles of "couverture" chocolate (a high quality chocolate that contains extra cocoa butter).

For more refined chocolate, choose specialist shops and health-food shops or internet suppliers who may have a wider range, favouring quality production and chocolates with a higher cocoa content, up to as much as 100% cocoa.

14

Where does chocolate come from?

By Laurence Alemanno

Chocolate is made from the seeds of the cacao tree, also known as cocoa beans. After the pods have been gathered, the cocoa beans are extracted from them. They are fermented for a few days to encourage their aroma precursors to synthesize, then dried in the sun.

At this stage the beans are sold and sent to the consumer countries, which are also the main countries where chocolate is made. The beans are then roasted to develop the chocolate flavour. Their shells are removed before they are ground and become the cocoa mass which is indispensable in the making of dark chocolate, milk chocolate and even white chocolate.

If the cocoa mass is pressed, cocoa fat is extracted: this is cocoa butter. It is by adding sugar and powdered milk to the cocoa butter that white chocolate is obtained. Dark chocolate is made directly from the cocoa mass to which sugar and cocoa butter are added. Milk chocolate is also made from the cocoa mass into which cocoa butter, powdered milk and sugar are incorporated.

When choosing dark chocolate, two criteria should be taken into account: the chocolate's percentage and the origin of the cocoa beans.

The higher the chocolate's percentage, the more cocoa mass and the more cocoa butter it contains, and the less sugar. From the point of view of taste, a chocolate with a high percentage will be less sweet and more intense than a chocolate with a low percentage.

The origin of the cocoa beans is very important for the final taste. Today, 50 countries produce cocoa. Depending on the varieties grown and the place where they are grown, the chocolate will have a different taste. So very roughly we can distinguish common cocoa (which has a basic pronounced chocolate taste) from fine aromatic cocoas. As well as the chocolate aroma, these have more subtle flavours: fresh fruit aromas for Madagascar cocoa, floral aromas for the Nacional Arriba from Ecuador for example. The origin of the cocoa beans is rarely mentioned on the most common brands of chocolate bars. However, whenever you are dealing with a quality chocolate or an organic or fair trade chocolate, the origin is specified. It is up to you to taste and choose the chocolate that suits you best!

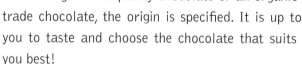

"Chocolate is a divine, celestial drink, the sweat of
the stars, the vital seed, divine nectar,
the drink of the Gods, panacea and universal medicine."
(Geronimo Piperni, quoted by Antonio Lavedán,
surgeon in the Spanish army, 1796)

16 ❖ Dark chocolate with cocoa beans

Remove the outer skin from each cocoa bean. Grind them roughly in a mortar so that you have some crunchy pieces.

Melt the dark chocolate using a bain-marie. Stir constantly until you have a smooth consistency, or temper the chocolate according to the method described on pages 11 and 12 (tempering).

Add about ¾ of the pieces of cocoa bean to the chocolate and mix together.

Pour the chocolate into a chocolate bar mould.

Smooth by gently shaking the mould from side to side.

Sprinkle the rest of the pieces of cocoa bean on top.

Leave, uncovered, in a cold place (refrigerator) for at least 3 hours.

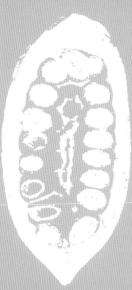

Ingredients

- 90g 75% cocoa dark chocolate pistoles
- 10g unroasted cocoa beans*

*Cocoa beans can be found in specialist chocolate shops or some health-food shops.

"I must have been ten years old – maybe older – before I first tasted real chocolate. But still the fascination endured."
(Joanne Harris, *Chocolat*)

18 ❖ Dark chocolate with a seed and berry mix

Melt the dark chocolate using a bain-marie. Stir constantly until you have a smooth consistency, or temper the chocolate according to the method described on pages 11 and 12 (tempering).

Add half of the seed and berry mix to the hot chocolate and mix together.

Pour into a chocolate bar mould so that the seeds and berries are evenly distributed. Smooth by gently shaking the mould from side to side.

While the chocolate is still warm, stick the rest of the dried berries and seeds upright into it.

Leave, uncovered, in a cold place (refrigerator) for at least 3 hours.

 Ingredients

- 60g dark chocolate
- 30g mixed seeds and berries: sunflower seeds, pumpkin seeds, pine nuts, dried berries (cranberries, blackberries and goji berries)

19 ❖ Dark chocolate with chickpeas and mallow flowers

Heat the chickpeas in a frying pan with the honey on a medium heat for about 4 minutes until the chickpeas turn brown. Turn off the heat and leave the chickpeas to cool.

Melt the dark chocolate using a bain-marie. Stir constantly until you have a smooth consistency, or temper the chocolate according to the method described on pages 11 and 12 (tempering).

Set aside 5 or 6 chickpeas. Add the rest of the chickpeas to the chocolate and stir.

Pour the chocolate into a chocolate bar mould with the chickpeas evenly distributed. Smooth by gently shaking the mould from side to side. Scatter the extra chickpeas on top along with the mallow flowers.

Leave, uncovered, in a cold place (refrigerator) for at least 3 hours.

 Ingredients

- 90g dark chocolate
- 5g white chickpeas
- 1 dessertspoon honey
- 1 teaspoon dried mallow flowers

"There are four basic food groups: milk chocolate, dark chocolate, white chocolate and chocolate truffles."
(Anonymous)

20   Dark chocolate with lemon curd

Melt half of the dark chocolate (45g) using a bain-marie. Stir constantly until you have a smooth consistency, or temper the chocolate according to the method described on pages 11 and 12 (tempering).

Pour into a chocolate bar mould and spread out this first layer of chocolate. Place in the freezer for 10 minutes.

Remove the chocolate mould from the freezer and spread the lemon curd on the chocolate, using a teaspoon to make this layer as smooth as possible.

Put the chocolat bar mould in the freezer for 3 minutes.

Melt the rest of the chocolate according to the same method as before and pour it on top.

Smooth by gently shaking the mould from side to side.

Leave, uncovered, in a cold place (refrigerator) for at least 3 hours.

Lemon curd:

Grate the lemons very finely using just enough pressure to remove the thin top layer of the zest.

Squeeze the juice out of the lemons.

Mix all the ingredients together in a small saucepan or bowl then heat gently using a bain-marie over a low flame, stirring constantly until the lemon curd has a smooth, thick consistency.

Let the lemon curd cool at room temperature.

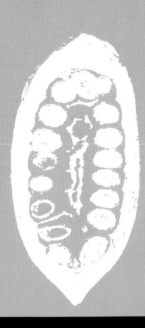

Ingredients

- 90g dark chocolate
- 35g lemon curd

Lemon curd:
- 2 eggs
- 50g sugar
- 25g butter
- 2 lemons (preferably unwaxed or organic) for their juice and zest

"Money talks. Chocolate sings."
(Anonymous)

22 ❖ Dark chocolate, milk chocolate and grilled almonds

Melt the dark chocolate using a bain-marie. Stir constantly until you have a smooth consistency, or temper the chocolate according to the method described on pages 11 and 12 (tempering).

Pour into a chocolate bar mould, then spread this first layer of chocolate out and place in the freezer for 10 minutes.

Roast the almonds in a frying pan or under the grill until they turn golden.

Spread them in a second layer over the dark chocolate.

Melt the milk chocolate using a bain-marie according to the same method as above and pour it onto the almonds.

Smooth by gently shaking the mould from side to side.

Leave, uncovered, in a cold place (refrigerator) for at least 3 hours.

Ingredients

- 40g dark chocolate
- 50g milk chocolate
- 5g slivered almonds

Cranberries grow mainly in North America.

23 ❖ Dark chocolate with dried cranberries and slivered almonds

Melt the dark chocolate using a bain-marie. Stir constantly until you have a smooth consistency, or temper the chocolate according to the method described on pages 11 and 12 (tempering).

Add the cranberries.

Pour half of the chocolate mixture into the chocolate bar mould and keep the rest warm in the pan.

Scatter half of the slivered almonds as a second layer.

Pour the rest of the chocolate mixture on top.

Smooth by gently shaking the mould from side to side.

Sprinkle the rest of the almonds on top.

Leave, uncovered, in a cold place (refrigerator) for at least 3 hours.

 Ingredients

- 80g dark chocolate
- 10g dried cranberries
- 5g slivered almonds

"Twill make Old Women Young and Fresh,
Create New Motions of the Flesh,
And cause them long for you know what,
If they but taste of Chocolate."
(James Wadworth, 1768–1844,
A History of the Nature and Quality of Chocolate)

24 ❖ Dark chocolate with physalis

Remove the stalks from the physalis.

Melt the dark chocolate using a bain-marie. Stir constantly until you have a smooth consistency, or temper the chocolate according to the method described on pages 11 and 12 (tempering).

Pour the chocolate into a chocolate bar mould.

Smooth by gently shaking the mould from side to side.

Cool for about 15 minutes at room temperature.

Place the physalis, one by one, on the surface of the chocolate.

Leave, uncovered, in a cold place (refrigerator) for at least 3 hours.

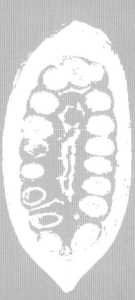

Ingredients

- 80g dark chocolate
- 7 physalis

Dark chocolate lollipop with Fleur de sel

Melt the dark chocolate using a bain-marie. Stir constantly until you have a smooth consistency, or temper the chocolate according to the method described on pages 11 and 12 (tempering).

Add 10 Fleur de sel crystals to the pan and mix.

Pour the chocolate into a silicone tartlet tin.

Smooth by gently shaking the mould from side to side.

Scatter the remaining 5 salt crystals on top.

Leave, uncovered, in a cold place (refrigerator) for at least 3 hours.

 ## Ingredients

For one lollipop:
- 40g dark chocolate
- 15 Fleur de sel crystals (French sea salt)
- 1 lollipop stick

 # Fresh basil lollipop

Set aside the prettiest basil leaf for decoration.

Roughly chop the other 6 leaves with a knife.

Melt the dark chocolate using a bain-marie. Stir constantly until you have a smooth consistency, or temper the chocolate according to the method described on pages 11 and 12 (tempering).

Add the chopped basil and mix. Pour the mixture into a silicone tartlet tin. Smooth by gently shaking the tin from side to side.

While the chocolate is still warm, place the whole basil leaf on top.

Leave, uncovered, in a cold place (refrigerator) for at least 3 hours.

 ## Ingredients

For one lollipop:
- 40g dark chocolate
- 7 fine fresh basil leaves (about 3g)
- 1 lollipop stick

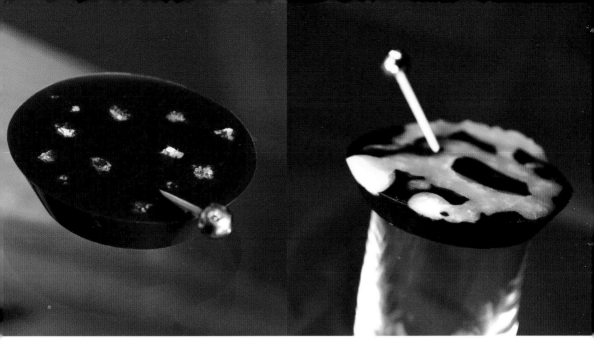

27 ❖ Dark chocolate lollipop with lemon curd glaze

Melt the dark chocolate using a bain-marie. Stir constantly until you have a smooth consistency, or temper the chocolate according to the method described on pages 11 and 12 (tempering).

Pour the chocolate into a silicone tartlet tin.

Make caramel with the sugar and water. Add the lemon curd and heat for 3 minutes, stirring constantly.

Pour the lemon curd caramel onto the chocolate in an uneven layer.

Leave, uncovered, in a cold place (refrigerator) for at least 3 hours.

 Ingredients

For one lollipop:
- 25g dark chocolate
- 1 dessertspoon lemon curd (see page 20)
- 15g sugar
- 15g water
- 1 lollipop stick

"The raw and earthy tang of the Americas, the hot and resinous perfumes of the rainforest."
(Joanne Harris, *Chocolat*)

28 ❖ Strong dark chocolate with green cardamom

Remove the seeds from the cardamom by making a slit along the length of the pod with the point of a knife. Scrape the inside to retrieve the seeds.

Melt the dark chocolate using a bain-marie. Stir constantly until you have a smooth consistency, or temper the chocolate according to the method described on pages 11 and 12 (tempering).

Add the cardamom seeds to the hot chocolate and stir.

Pour into a chocolate bar mould.

Smooth by gently shaking the mould from side to side.

Leave, uncovered, in a cold place (refrigerator) for at least 3 hours.

*Green cardamom is a dried fruit found as a grey-green pod with three compartments containing dark brown seeds which are the only aromatic parts.

Cardamom has a very strong but not "hot" flavour.

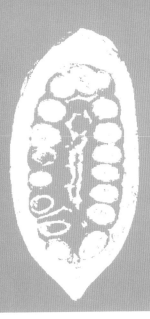

Ingredients

- 90g strong dark chocolate
  (64% cocoa minimum)
- 20g green cardamom pods*

"Chocolate is a perfect food, as wholesome as it is delicious, a
beneficent restorer of exhausted power ... it is the best friend
of those engaged in literary pursuits."
(Baron Justus von Liebig, German chemist, 1803–1873)

30 ❖ Dark chocolate with Espelette pepper

Melt the dark chocolate using a bain-marie. Stir constantly until you have a smooth consistency, or temper the chocolate according to the method described on pages 11 and 12 (tempering).

Add 2g of Espelette pepper and stir.

Pour into a chocolate bar mould.

Smooth by gently shaking the mould from side to side.

Sprinkle the rest of the Espelette pepper on top.

Leave, uncovered, in a cold place (refrigerator) for at least 3 hours.

*Espelette pepper is a chili pepper from the French Basque countryside.

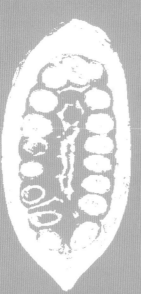

Ingredients

- 90g 70% dark chocolate
- 3g powdered Espelette pepper*

32 ❖ Dark chocolate with pasteli

Roughly chop the pasteli with a knife and keep the pieces.

Melt the dark chocolate using a bain-marie. Stir constantly until you have a smooth consistency, or temper the chocolate according to the method described on pages 11 and 12 (tempering).

Tip three quarters of the pieces of pasteli into the chocolate and stir.

Pour into a chocolate bar mould.

Smooth by gently shaking the mould from side to side.

Scatter the remaining pieces of pasteli on top.

Leave, uncovered, in a cold place (refrigerator) for at least 3 hours.

*Pasteli is a Greek sesame seed and honey brittle. It can be bought in specialist shops.

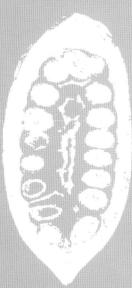

Ingredients

- 70g dark chocolate
- 25g pasteli*

"Forget about falling in love ... I'd rather fall in chocolate."
(Anonymous)

34 ❖ Dark chocolate with toffee

Melt the dark chocolate using a bain-marie. Stir constantly until you have a smooth consistency, or temper the chocolate according to the method described on pages 11 and 12 (tempering).

Pour into the chocolate bar mould and place in refrigerator for at least 2 minutes.

Place the toffee and the milk in a bowl (or a small container). Place the bowl in the microwave oven on high for 2 minutes. Then stir with a spoon to make a soft smooth toffee (heat again if the toffee is too hard).

Using a dessertspoon gradually pour the toffee on to the chocolate, making a pattern as desired.

Leave, uncovered, in a cold place (refrigerator) for at least 3 hours.

*The Carambar brand is the fourth-largest confectionery line in France.

Ingredients

- 90g dark chocolate
- 4 caramel Carambars® or about 30g of toffee*
- 400ml semi-skimmed milk

"All I really need is love, but a little chocolate now and then doesn't hurt."
(Lucy Van Pelt in *Peanuts* by Charles M. Schulz)

35 ❖ Milk or dark chocolate with whole hazelnuts

Melt the milk chocolate using a bain-marie. Stir constantly until you have a smooth consistency, or temper the chocolate according to the method described on pages 11 and 12 (tempering).

Mix half of the hazelnuts into the chocolate.

Pour into a chocolate bar mould, evenly distributing the hazelnuts.

While the chocolate is still warm, scatter the rest of the hazelnuts on top, pushing them more or less deeply into the chocolate according to the appearance you want to give to the bar (whole hazelnuts more or less visible).

Leave, uncovered, in a cold place (refrigerator) for at least 3 hours.

Ingredients

- 70g milk or dark chocolate
- 20g whole hazelnuts

"If I have chocolate around, I will eat it. I love it,
I love it, I love it. I like a piece every day."
(Julia Louis-Dreyfus)

36 ❖ Strong dark chocolate with tamarind

Break the outer pods of the tamarinds and remove the fruity pulp. Remove the strands of fibre around the pulp. Using a knife, take out the seeds that are inside the pulp. Dice the pulp and set aside 50g.

Melt the dark chocolate using a bain-marie. Stir constantly until you have a smooth consistency, or temper the chocolate according to the method described on pages 11 and 12 (tempering).

Add the diced pieces of fruity pulp and mix.

Pour into a chocolate bar mould, evenly distributing the pieces of tamarind pulp.

Smooth by gently shaking the mould from side to side.

Leave, uncovered, in a cold place (refrigerator) for at least 3 hours.

*Tamarind is a tropical fruit originally from India. It comes as a brown pod containing a fruity pulp with la number of seeds embedded in the pulp. Often made into a paste, it may be used as a slightly acidic spice, with a lemony taste.

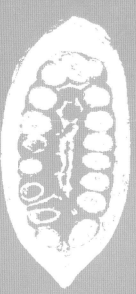

Ingredients

- 70g dark chocolate
- 100g whole tamarinds*
  (or 50g tamarind pulp)

38 ❖ Dark chocolate with pieces of nougatine

Melt the dark chocolate using a bain-marie. Stir constantly until you have a smooth consistency, or temper the chocolate according to the method described on pages 11 and 12 (tempering).

Add three quarters of the pieces of nougatine to the chocolate and mix well. Pour into a chocolate bar mould.

Smooth by gently shaking the mould from side to side.

Scatter the rest of the nougatine on top.

Leave, uncovered, in a cold place (refrigerator) for at least 3 hours.

Nougatine:

Grind the almonds and the hazelnuts in a food-processor for 1 minute so as not to reduce them all to powder but keep some pieces.

In a saucepan, heat the sugar and the water rapidly to make a caramel, stirring constantly. When it has reached the desired consistency and colour, pour in a little cold water and stir. Pour the almond and hazelnut mixture into the caramel immediately and stir to obtain a nougatine with the nuts evenly distributed.

Cut out two pieces of baking parchment (at least 20 cm square). Lay one square out flat and immediately pour the hot nougatine onto it. Place the other square of paper on top and use a rolling pin to roll out the nougatine as thinly as possible. Remove the baking parchment and leave to cool for a few minutes.

The preparation of the nougatine should be done rapidly so as to be able to work it before the caramel solidifies.

Once the nougatine is hard, break it up into pieces.

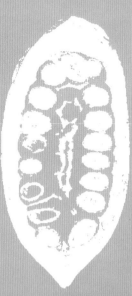

Ingredients

- 90g dark chocolate
- 30g nougatine

For 30g nougatine:
- 15g whole almonds
- 15g whole hazelnuts
- 50g sugar
- 4 dessertspoons water

40 Dark chocolate with crystallised mango and crêpe dentelle biscuits

Cut the mango into very small cubes (about 2mm).

Melt the dark chocolate using a bain-marie. Stir constantly until you have a smooth consistency, or temper the chocolate according to the method described on pages 11 and 12 (tempering).

Add the cubes of mango and stir.

Pour a thin layer of chocolate into a chocolate bar mould, evenly distributing the pieces of mango, then scatter a thin layer of pieces of crêpe dentelle on top.

Repeat this to make a layered effect, ending with a layer of chocolate.

Smooth by gently shaking the mould from side to side.

Leave, uncovered, in a cold place (refrigerator) for at least 3 hours.

Ingredients

- 70g dark chocolate
- 10g crêpe dentelle biscuits (a lacy, paper-thin, crispy crepe biscuit from France)
- 7g crystallised mango

41 ❖ Dark chocolate with feuilles de brick and maple syrup

Toast the sheet of pastry in an ungreased frying pan (or under the oven grill) until it is golden and hard.

Leave to cool for a few minutes, then spread the maple syrup over the pastry with a pastry brush (or with your finger). Break off pieces of pastry about the size of the chocolate bar mould.

Melt the dark chocolate using a bain-marie. Stir constantly until you have a smooth consistency, or temper the chocolate according to the method described on pages 11 and 12 (tempering).

Once it is hot, pour about a third of the chocolate into the chocolate bar mould. Cover with overlapping pieces of pastry, completely covering the chocolate. Repeat this operation for two or three layers of pastry, then top with a layer of chocolate.

Leave, uncovered, in a cold place (refrigerator) for at least 3 hours.

 Ingredients

- 80g dark chocolate
- 1 sheet feuilles de brick pastry (Tunisian brick pastry – filo pastry can be used as an alternative)
- 1 dessertspoon maple syrup

"And outside the walls, for half a mile around
in every direction, the air was scented with
the heavy rich smell of melting chocolate."
(Roald Dahl, *Charlie and the Chocolate Factory*)

42 ❖ Dark chocolate with coffee and ginger

Peel the ginger and grate as finely as possible.

Melt the dark chocolate using a bain-marie. Stir constantly until you have a smooth consistency, or temper the chocolate according to the method described on pages 11 and 12 (tempering).

Add the coffee extract and the ginger.

Mix vigorously, then pour immediately into the chocolate bar mould (adding a liquid to the chocolate tends to make it solidify).

Leave, uncovered, in a cold place (refrigerator) for at least 3 hours.

Ingredients

- 90g strong dark chocolate (minimum 70%)
- 10 drops coffee extract
- 1g fresh ginger

"In the beginning the Lord created chocolate, and he saw it was good. Then he separated the light from the dark, and it was better. " (Anonymous)

43 ❖❖❖ White chocolate with coffee

Melt the white chocolate using a bain-marie. Stir constantly until you have a smooth consistency, or temper the chocolate according to the method described on pages 11 and 12 (tempering).

Turn off the heat.

Add the coffee granules to the chocolate and mix well (the coffee granules do not dissolve in the chocolate but remain whole).

Pour into a chocolate bar mould.

Smooth by gently shaking the mould from side to side.

Leave, uncovered, in a cold place (refrigerator) for at least 3 hours.

Ingredients

- 90g white chocolate
- 1 teaspoon instant coffee granules

44 ❖ Dark chocolate with lemon balm

Boil the water in a saucepan. Turn off the heat and add 1 dessertspoon of lemon balm leaves. Leave them to soak for at least 5 minutes. Drain them, then dry them by pressing gently with kitchen paper.

Melt the dark chocolate using a bain-marie. Stir constantly until you have a smooth consistency, or temper the chocolate according to the method described on pages 11 and 12 (tempering).

Turn off the heat and add the rehydrated lemon balm leaves.

Mix together vigorously and pour immediately into a chocolate bar mould.

Scatter the remaining dried lemon balm leaves on top.

Leave, uncovered, in a cold place (refrigerator) for at least 3 hours.

 Ingredients

- 90g dark chocolate
- 2 dessertspoons dried lemon balm leaves
- 250ml water

45 ❖ Dark chocolate with little Japanese coloured sweets

Melt the dark chocolate using a bain-marie. Stir constantly until you have a smooth consistency, or temper the chocolate according to the method described on pages 11 and 12 (tempering).

Pour into a chocolate bar mould.

Smooth by gently shaking the mould from side to side.

Scatter the sweets on top.

Leave, uncovered, in a cold place (refrigerator) for at least 3 hours.

 Ingredients

- 90g dark chocolate
- 7g little coloured sweets and matcha tea stars (instead of the Japanese sweets, coloured sugar strands may be used)

On St Valentine's Day the custom is for Japanese women
to give chocolates as a lover's gift to their fiancé or hus-
band, as a "bite of happiness" to their friends, and as a
tasty luxury gift to their superiors at work.

46 ❖ Strong dark chocolate with matcha tea

Melt the dark chocolate using a bain-marie. Stir constantly until
you have a smooth consistency, or temper the chocolate according
to the method described on pages 11 and 12 (tempering).

Turn off the heat and add half (ie 1 dessertspoon) of the matcha
tea powder, mixing well.

Pour into a chocolate bar mould.

Smooth by gently shaking the mould from side to side.

Leave to cool for at least 10 minutes. When the surface of the bar
is cool enough, sprinkle the rest of the tea powder on top.

Leave, uncovered, in a cold place (refrigerator) for at least 3 hours.

Useful tip: to know whether the surface of the chocolate is cool
enough so that the tea powder does not melt and keeps its pale
green colour, test it (several times if necessary) – if the powder
melts and turns dark green, put the chocolate bar back into the
refrigerator for a few minutes.

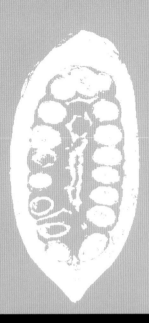

Ingredients

- 90g dark chocolate (strong, if you want a bitter chocolate bar)
- 2 dessertspoons matcha tea* powder

*Matcha is powdered green tea used for the Japanese tea ceremony and as a colouring or natural flavouring for cakes. Unlike other teas, matcha is not infused but has to be whipped in the hot water with a bamboo whisk (chasen) to make an emulsion.

The goji is a little red berry from Tibet, called the "longevity fruit" in the countries of Asia where it is consumed as a real health food. In Europe it can be found as juice or dried berries. These berries are known to be rich in vitamins, minerals and trace elements, and full of powerful antioxidants.

48 ❖ Dark chocolate with goji berries

Boil the water then turn off the heat.

Divide the goji berries into two portions.

Take the goji berries in the first portion and cut them all in two, putting them into a ramekin.

Pour the hot water on to the berries and leave them to soak for at least 15 minutes so as to rehydrate them.

Drain them and press gently between sheets of kitchen paper to remove as much liquid as possible.

Melt the dark chocolate using a bain-marie. Stir constantly until you have a smooth consistency, or temper the chocolate according to the method described on pages 11 and 12 (tempering).

Add the rehydrated goji berries.

Mix well and pour into a chocolate bar mould.

Smooth by gently shaking the mould from side to side.

Scatter the remaining dried goji berries on top.

Leave, uncovered, in a cold place (refrigerator) for at least 3 hours.

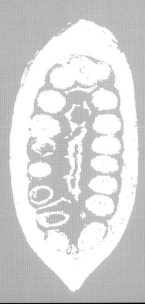

Ingredients

- 90g dark chocolate
- 2 dessertspoons goji berries
- 250ml water

50 ❖ Dark chocolate with meringue

Melt the dark chocolate using a bain-marie. Stir constantly until you have a smooth consistency, or temper the chocolate according to the method described on pages 11 and 12 (tempering).

Pour half of the chocolate into the chocolate bar mould to form a first layer.

Cut out a flat sheet of meringue the same size as the chocolate bar mould. Place it on top of the first layer of chocolate.

Pour the rest of the chocolate on top and smooth by gently shaking the mould from side to side.

Add a few rounds of meringue on top of the bar of chocolate.

Leave, uncovered, in a cold place (refrigerator) for at least 3 hours.

Variation:

Roughly break the meringue up into pieces.

Melt the dark chocolate using a bain-marie. Stir constantly until you have a smooth consistency, or temper the chocolate according to the method described on pages 11 and 12 (tempering).

Set aside some meringue crumbs and stir the rest into the chocolate. Pour into a chocolate bar mould.

Sprinkle the rest of the meringue crumbs on to the chocolate.

Leave, uncovered, in a cold place (refrigerator) for at least 3 hours.

Meringue:

Using a hand whisk, beat the egg whites till firm (do not use an electric beater as it will beat the eggs until they are too stiff), remembering to add a pinch of salt.

When the whites are firm but not too stiff, add the sugar. Mix together with a dessertspoon or a spatula folding the sugar in and taking care not to break up the beaten egg whites. Grease a baking tray with butter.

Make some round drops by letting ½ teaspoon of beaten egg white fall on to the tray (to decorate the top of the chocolate bar).

Spread the rest of the beaten egg white in a layer about 1 cm thick. Smooth the surface.

Bake in the oven at a low temperature (80°C) for about 45 to 60 minutes. The meringue should be hard on top but soft inside.

Leave to cool, then lift off the sheet of meringue and the round drops.

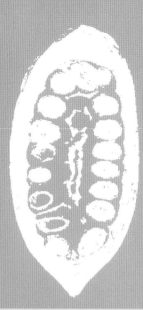

Ingredients

- 80g dark chocolate
- 15g meringue

Meringue:
- 150g sugar
- 3 egg whites
- 1 pinch salt
- 10g butter (to grease the baking tray)

52 ❖❖❖ Dark chocolate with butter cookies

Set aside one of the shaped butter cookies (see below) and break the rest up roughly into crumbs.

Melt the dark chocolate using a bain-marie. Stir constantly until you have a smooth consistency, or temper the chocolate according to the method described on pages 11 and 12 (tempering).

Pour the cookie crumbs into the hot chocolate and mix well.

Pour into a chocolate bar mould, evenly distributing the pieces of cookie.

Smooth by gently shaking the mould from side to side.

Place the shaped butter cookie on top.

Leave, uncovered, in a cold place (refrigerator) for at least 3 hours.

Butter cookies:

Melt the butter in a saucepan on a low heat.

Pour it into a large bowl and beat with a whisk for about one minute until it becomes creamy.

Add the sugar, salt and egg white. Beat for one minute, then gradually add the flour, stirring with a spatula or a spoon until the flour is well mixed in. The dough should be smooth, without lumps. Fill a piping bag fitted with a star-shaped tube with the dough.

Place a sheet of baking parchment on a baking tray. Make long, thin zigzags of cookie dough at least as long as the chocolate bar (or any other shape desired).

Place in a preheated oven (180°C/thermostat 6) and bake for 15 to 18 minutes.

Remove the cookies from the oven and leave to cool.

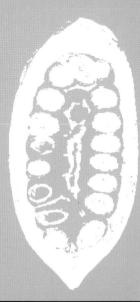

Ingredients

- 80g strong dark chocolate (minimum 70% cocoa)
- 15g butter cookies

Butter cookies:

- 60g white flour
- 50g butter
- 15g sugar
- 1 pinch salt
- 1 egg white

"Chocolate is quite obviously the stuff that dreams are
made of. Rich, dark, silky and soft dreams
that disturb the senses and awaken passion."
(Judith Olney, *The Joy of Chocolate*)

54 ❖ 100% dark chocolate with redcurrants

Remove the currants from their stalks.

Melt the dark chocolate using a bain-marie. Stir constantly until you have a smooth consistency, or temper the chocolate according to the method described on pages 11 and 12 (tempering).

Pour into a chocolate bar mould.

Smooth by gently shaking the mould from side to side.

Add the redcurrants one by one to the chocolate, placing them at regular intervals on the surface and pushing them partly into the chocolate so that they remain visible.

Leave, uncovered, in a cold place (refrigerator) for at least 3 hours.

Useful tip: you can also choose to push each currant right into the chocolate so that it is hidden. This produces an even greater surprise when a currant is bitten into.

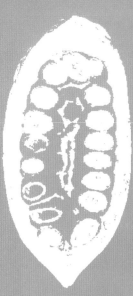

Ingredients

- 90g dark chocolate (100% cocoa*)
- about 20g fresh redcurrants (between 18 and 20 currants)

The bitterness of the strong chocolate goes marvellously well with the juicy acid flavour of the redcurrants.

*100% chocolate is rare but can be found in specialist shops and delicatessens.

"So noble a confection, more than nectar and ambrosia, the true food of the gods."
(Dr Bachot, 1662))

56 ❖ Dark chocolate with golden oat flakes

Put the oat flakes and the butter in a frying pan. Gently toast the oats on a low heat for about 5 minutes until they are nicely golden. Leave them to cool uncovered for at least 2 hours (so that the flakes dry out slightly).

Melt the dark chocolate using a bain-marie. Stir constantly until you have a smooth consistency, or temper the chocolate according to the method described on pages 11 and 12 (tempering).

Pour half of the flakes into the hot chocolate and mix well. Pour into a chocolate bar mould.

Smooth by gently shaking the mould from side to side. Scatter the rest of the oat flakes on the surface of the chocolate.

Leave, uncovered, in a cold place (refrigerator) for at least 3 hours.

 Ingredients

- 90g dark chocolate (at least 60%)
- 7g oat flakes
- 10g unsalted butter

"If I was the headmaster of a school, I would get rid of the history teacher and replace him with a chocolate teacher: my pupils would at least be studying a subject that is of interest to them all."
(Roald Dahl)

57 ❖ Dark chocolate with red pralines

Melt the dark chocolate using a bain-marie. Stir constantly until you have a smooth consistency, or temper the chocolate according to the method described on pages 11 and 12 (tempering).

Pour into a chocolate bar mould.

Smooth by gently shaking the mould from side to side.

Evenly distribute the red pralines and push them gently into the chocolate.

Leave, uncovered, in a cold place (refrigerator) for at least 3 hours.

Ingredients

- 80g dark chocolate
- 10 to 12 red pralines (about 30g depending on their size). Red pralines are roasted almonds covered in red sugar paste.

58 ❖ Dark chocolate with caramel bubbles

Put the sugar and the water in a small saucepan and heat gently until the sugar dissolves then bring to the boil to make the caramel. Stir constantly.

When it has reached the desired consistency and colour, remove the pan from the heat.

Lay out a sheet of aluminium foil flat and pour the hot caramel on to it immediately, using a small spoon to make the caramel fall in small drops.

Leave it to cool.

Meanwhile, melt the dark chocolate using a bain-marie. Stir constantly until you have a smooth consistency, or temper the chocolate according to the method described on pages 11 and 12 (tempering).

Pour into a chocolate bar mould.

Smooth by gently shaking the mould from side to side.

Leave it to cool at room temperature for about 10 minutes.

Carefully place the caramel bubbles on the chocolate.

Leave, uncovered, in a cold place (refrigerator) for at least 3 hours.

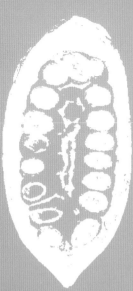

Ingredients

- 90g dark chocolate
- 100g sugar
- 40ml water

"The first fragment of chocolate had melted on Winston's tongue. The taste was delightful."
(George Orwell, *1984*)

60 ❖ Black and white chocolate

Melt the dark chocolate using a bain-marie. Stir constantly until you have a smooth consistency, or temper the chocolate according to the method described on pages 11 and 12 (tempering).

Pour into a chocolate bar mould. Smooth by gently shaking the mould from side to side.

Melt the white chocolate using a bain-marie in the same way.

Using a dessertspoon, put the white chocolate in a piping bag fitted with a tube with a wide slit.

Pipe the white chocolate onto the dark in wide question mark shapes (or any other shape).

Leave, uncovered, in a cold place (refrigerator) for at least 3 hours.

 Ingredients

- 60g dark chocolate (70%)
- 30g white chocolate

"I carried recipes in my head like maps."
(Joanne Harris, *Chocolat*)

61 ❖ Dark chocolate with fresh coconut

Cut the coconut into small cubes (about 2 to 3mm), removing the fine brown skin.

Melt the dark chocolate using a bain-marie. Stir constantly until you have a smooth consistency, or temper the chocolate according to the method described on pages 11 and 12 (tempering).

Place half of the coconut cubes in the chocolate and mix well. Pour into a chocolate bar mould.

Smooth by gently shaking the mould from side to side.

One by one, place the remaining cubes of coconut, evenly distributed, on the surface of the chocolate.

Leave, uncovered, in a cold place (refrigerator) for at least 3 hours.

 Ingredients

- 80g dark chocolate
- 20g fresh coconut

"Les longs cheveux de ma mère
et les joues de mon papa,
les matins dans la lumière,
la rose et le chocolat."
(Pierre Gamarra, *Mon cartable*)

62 ❖ Dark chocolate with rose petals

Bring the water to the boil. Once it is boiling, remove the saucepan from the heat.

Immediately add 2 dessertspoons of rose petals to the water and leave them to soak for at least 1 hour.

Drain, then press the petals gently between sheets of kitchen paper to remove as much liquid as possible.

Melt the dark chocolate using a bain-marie. Stir constantly until you have a smooth consistency, or temper the chocolate according to the method described on pages 11 and 12 (tempering).

Turn off the heat, add the petals and the rose water to the chocolate and stir vigorously.

Pour into a chocolate bar mould immediately.

Smooth by gently shaking the mould from side to side (and, if necessary, use a long-bladed knife).

Scatter the rest of the dried rose petals on top.

Leave, uncovered, in a cold place (refrigerator) for at least 3 hours.

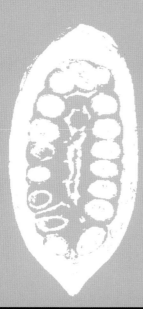

Ingredients

- 90g dark chocolate
- 3 dessertspoons of dried rose petals: 2 dessertspoons to mix into the chocolate and 1 dessertspoon for decoration
- 1 teaspoon rose water
- 200ml water

64 ❖ Dark chocolate with dried pears and liquorice

Set aside the slice of dried whole pear and cut the 20g dried pear into small cubes of about 4 to 5mm.

Use a grater to grate the liquorice stick very finely so as to have a teaspoon of powder.

Melt the dark chocolate using a bain-marie. Stir constantly until you have a smooth consistency, or temper the chocolate according to the method described on pages 11 and 12 (tempering).

Add half a teaspoon of the grated liquorice and the cubes of dried pear. Mix well and pour into a chocolate bar mould.

Smooth by gently shaking the mould from side to side.

Place the slice of dried pear on top of the chocolate then sprinkle with the remaining half teaspoon of liquorice.

Leave, uncovered, in a cold place (refrigerator) for at least 3 hours.

Dried pears:

One pear is enough for the recipe. Choose an organic pear if possible as it is used unpeeled. Wash and dry it.

Cut it vertically into 2 to 3mm slices.

Lay these slices of pear flat on a baking tray covered with baking parchment.

Put in the oven and leave to dry at 80°C for at least an hour. The cooking time depends on the variety of pear chosen and its ripeness. The riper the pear is, the more juice it will produce and the longer the time needed for it to dry out.

The slices of pear should be slightly golden and have a rather hard, dry consistency. Leave to cool.

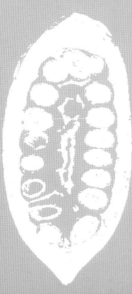

Ingredients

- 70g dark chocolate
- 20g dried pear + 1 whole slice of dried pear
- 1 small liquorice stick (enough for 1 teaspoon of grated liquorice)

66 ❖ Dark chocolate with dried kiwi fruit and rosemary

Select the biggest slice of kiwi fruit. Using a sharp knife, cut along the outside edge rotating the slice as you go so that you have a long rounded strip of kiwi fruit (like peeling fruit).

Cut the rest of the kiwi fruit into 3 to 4mm cubes.

Chop 3 blades of rosemary very finely and mix them with the cubes of kiwi fruit.

Melt the dark chocolate using a bain-marie. Stir constantly until you have a smooth consistency, or temper the chocolate according to the method described on pages 11 and 12 (tempering).

Add the cubes of kiwi fruit and rosemary to the chocolate and mix well.

Pour into a chocolate bar mould, evenly distributing the cubes of kiwi fruit.

Smooth by gently shaking the mould from side to side.

Cool for about 10 minutes at room temperature.

Lay the "rosette" of kiwi fruit on top along with the two remaining blades of rosemary.

Leave, uncovered, in a cold place (refrigerator) for at least 3 hours.

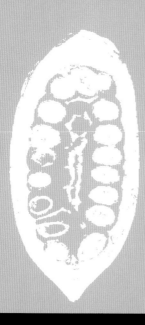

Ingredients

- 80g dark chocolate
- 3 large slices dried kiwi fruit (about 20g)
- 5 blades fresh rosemary

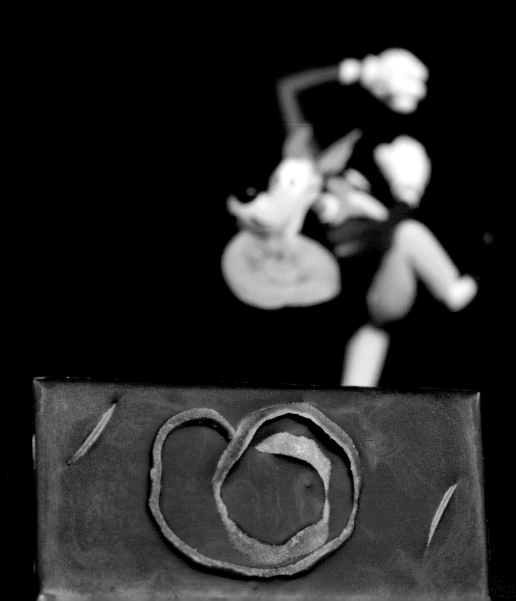

> "In my dreams I gorge on chocolates, I roll in
> chocolates, and their texture is not brittle but
> soft as flesh, like a thousand mouths on my body,
> devouring me in fluttering small bites."
> (Joanne Harris, *Chocolat*)

68 ❖ Dark chocolate with dried bananas

Cut the dried bananas into approximately 3mm thick slices (slightly on the diagonal so as to have fairly large strips).

Melt the dark chocolate using a bain-marie. Stir constantly until you have a smooth consistency, or temper the chocolate according to the method described on pages 11 and 12 (tempering).

Set aside 5 or 6 strips of banana, then add the rest to the chocolate and mix well.

Pour into a chocolate bar mould.

Smooth by gently shaking the mould from side to side.

Place the rest of the strips of banana in a semi-circle on top of the chocolate.

Leave, uncovered, in a cold place (refrigerator) for at least 3 hours.

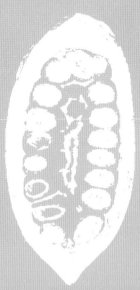

Ingredients

- 80g dark chocolate
- 20g whole dried bananas

70 ❖ Dark chocolate with smoked sencha tea

Bring the water to the boil. Place the dried sencha tea in the water, mix and let it infuse for at least 2 hours.

Drain, then press the tea gently between sheets of kitchen paper to remove as much liquid as possible.

Roughly chop 4g of sencha tea leaves to mix with the chocolate.

Melt the dark chocolate using a bain-marie. Stir constantly until you have a smooth consistency, or temper the chocolate according to the method described on pages 11 and 12 (tempering).

Add the 4g of chopped tea leaves to the hot chocolate and mix well.

Pour into a chocolate bar mould.

Smooth by gently shaking the mould from side to side.

Leave, uncovered, in a cold place (refrigerator) for at least 3 hours.

Suggested presentation:

Pour the chocolate into small silicone cake or biscuit tins with a little wooden lollipop stick in each.

 Ingredients

- 80g dark chocolate
- 4 dessertspoons dried sencha tea*
- 250ml water

*Sencha tea is a green tea. It represents three quarters of Japan's tea production. This roasted tea gives off a strong smoky aroma and has a characteristic leafy flavour.

71 ❖ Dark chocolate with figs and bergamot tea

Bring the water to the boil, then let the sachet of bergamot tea infuse for at least 5 minutes so as to get a strong infusion.

Scrape the inside of the figs with a round-ended knife to remove the flesh (the skins can be discarded).

Add the flesh of the figs to the tea, mix well and leave to soak for at least 1 hour.

Then drain the fig flesh and remove any remaining pieces of skin and any hard parts. Press it gently with the back of a dessertspoon to make a rather liquid paste. Set aside 30g of fig paste.

Melt the dark chocolate using a bain-marie. Stir constantly until you have a smooth consistency, or temper the chocolate according to the method described on pages 11 and 12 (tempering).

Pour half of the chocolate into the chocolate bar mould. Spread it out and smooth this first layer by gently shaking the mould from side to side. Let it cool in the freezer for 4 minutes.

Using a teaspoon, spread a layer of fig paste on top of the chocolate.

Pour the rest of the chocolate on top.

Smooth by gently shaking the mould from side to side.

Leave, uncovered, in a cold place (refrigerator) for at least 3 hours.

 Ingredients

- 70g dark chocolate
- 50g dried figs
- 1 sachet of bergamot tea
- 400ml water

The village of Ravello on the Amalfi coast is reputed for its production of Limoncello. Fields of lemon trees stretch up the hillsides overlooking the sea. Nets which catch the hailstones shelter very special lemons called *sfusato* ("balls of wool"). These big lemons are elongated and picked very green. Their flesh which is very acid is not used but their very thick skin is turned into an excellent limoncello. The amazingly sweet taste of the skin means it can also be eaten raw!

72 ❖ Dark chocolate with limoncello

Melt the dark chocolate using a bain-marie. Stir constantly until you have a smooth consistency, or temper the chocolate according to the method described on pages 11 and 12 (tempering).

Turn off the heat and add the limoncello all at once.

Mix vigorously so that the chocolate does not solidify.

Pour into a silicone muffin pan.

Smooth by gently shaking the mould from side to side.

Leave, uncovered, in a cold place (refrigerator) for at least 3 hours.

Limoncello:

Peel the lemons and keep only the skin.

In a large container soften the lemon peel in the alcohol for 4 days. Close the container hermetically and shake the liquid every day. After these 4 days filter the liquid through a fine sieve to remove the skin and other residue.

Make a syrup with the water and the sugar by heating the mixture on a low flame. Then leave to cool. When the syrup is cold, mix it with the filtered alcohol. Store in a cool place.

Decorate with a "ring" of crystallised lemon peel:

Remove the stalk from a lime.

Take a strip of crystallised lemon peel, twist it into a circle with the two ends overlapping.

To keep the circle's shape, push the lime stalk into the overlapping ends.

Place this "ring" on the chocolate when ready to serve.

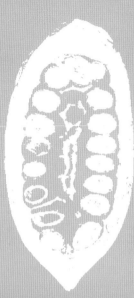

Ingredients

- 90g dark chocolate
- 30ml limoncello

Limoncello:

- 4 unwaxed or organic yellow lemons
- ½ l of 95% alcohol for fruit
- 500g sugar
- ½ l water

Decoration:

- 1 strip crystallised lemon peel
- 1 stalk from a lime (small, star-shaped stalk attached to the lime's skin)

74 ❖ Dark chocolate with whisky

Melt the dark chocolate using a bain-marie. Stir constantly until you have a smooth consistency, or temper the chocolate according to the method described on pages 11 and 12 (tempering).

Remove the pan from the heat and add the whisky all at once.

Mix vigorously so that the chocolate does not solidify because of the alcohol.

Pour into a chocolate bar mould.

Smooth by gently shaking the mould from side to side.

Leave, uncovered, in a cold place (refrigerator) for at least 3 hours.

NB: With this amount of whisky you will get a rather strong alcoholic chocolate. You can reduce the amount of whisky if you prefer a lighter chocolate.

 Ingredients

- 90g dark chocolate
- 12ml whisky

75 ❖❖❖ Dark chocolate with raisins and red wine

Cut the raisins in two. Put them in a small bowl and cover them with the red wine. Let them soften for 15 minutes.

Drain the raisins and press them gently with a dessertspoon to remove the excess wine.

Melt the dark chocolate using a bain-marie. Stir constantly until you have a smooth consistency, or temper the chocolate according to the method described on pages 11 and 12 (tempering).

Turn off the heat and rapidly mix the raisins with the melted chocolate. Pour the mixture into the chocolate bar mould immediately, evenly distributing the raisins.

Smooth the surface with a long-bladed knife and by gently shaking the mould from side to side.

Leave, uncovered, in a cold place (refrigerator) for at least 3 hours.

 Ingredients

- 80g dark chocolate
- 10g fat raisins
- 200ml red wine (eg Bordeaux)

76 ❖ Strong dark chocolate with ginger-flavoured crystallised lemon peel

Cut a few strips of the ginger-flavoured crystallised lemon peel, all the same length, for the decoration.

Thinly dice the rest of the crystallised lemon peel into 3mm cubes.

Melt the dark chocolate using a bain-marie. Stir constantly until you have a smooth consistency, or temper the chocolate according to the method described on pages 11 and 12 (tempering).

Add the cubes of lemon to the hot chocolate and mix well.

Pour into a chocolate bar mould.

Smooth by gently shaking the mould from side to side.

Place the strips of lemon diagonally across the top of the chocolate at regular intervals.

Leave, uncovered, in a cold place (refrigerator) for at least 3 hours.

Ginger-flavoured crystallised lemon peel:

Using a knife, peel the lemons and keep the skin.

Peel and roughly grate the ginger.

In a saucepan mix the sugar, water, lemon peel and ginger. Heat on a low flame. Leave it to crystallise for at least an hour, stirring every 10 minutes and adding water if the syrup becomes too thick.

Remove the lemon peel from the syrup and leave to drain on a rack.

(You can keep the syrup which can be used in the recipe on the next page.)

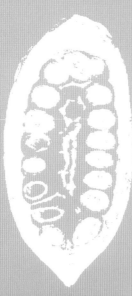

Ingredients

- 90g strong dark chocolate (minimum 70% cocoa)
- 20g ginger-flavoured crystallised lemon peel

Ginger-flavoured crystallised lemon peel:
- 2 lemons (preferably unwaxed or organic)
- 15g fresh ginger
- 70g sugar
- 700ml water

"Strength is the capacity to break a chocolate bar
into four pieces with your bare hands and
then to eat just one of the pieces."
(Judith Viorst))

78 ❖ Dark chocolate with lemon-and-ginger caramelised cornflakes

Mix the cornflakes and the syrup so that the flakes are covered in syrup.

Melt the dark chocolate using a bain-marie. Stir constantly until you have a smooth consistency, or temper the chocolate according to the method described on pages 11 and 12 (tempering).

Turn off the heat. Add three quarters of the cornflakes and mix well.

Pour into a chocolate bar mould, evenly distributing the flakes.

Smooth by gently shaking the mould from side to side.

Scatter the remaining flakes on top.

Leave, uncovered, in a cold place (refrigerator) for at least 3 hours.

Lemon and ginger syrup:

Using a knife, peel the lemons and keep the skin.

Peel and roughly grate the ginger.

In a saucepan mix the sugar, water, lemon peel and ginger. Heat on a low flame.

Leave the peel to crystallise for at least an hour, stirring every 10 minutes and adding water if the syrup becomes too thick.

Remove the lemon peel (which can be used in the recipe on page 76) and keep the syrup.

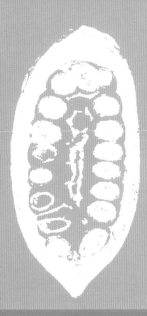

Ingredients

- 80g dark chocolate
- 3 dessertspoons unsweetened cornflakes
- 4 dessertspoons lemon and ginger syrup

Lemon and ginger syrup:
- 2 lemons (preferably unwaxed or organic)
- 15g fresh ginger
- 70g sugar
- 700ml water

"If at first you don't succeed, have a little chocolate." ⊙
(Anonymous)

80 ❖ Dark chocolate with lemon pepper

Melt the dark chocolate using a bain-marie. Stir constantly until you have a smooth consistency, or temper the chocolate according to the method described on pages 11 and 12 (tempering).

Pour into a chocolate bar mould.

Smooth by gently shaking the mould from side to side.

Leave in a cold place for at least 10 minutes.

When the surface has solidified enough, sprinkle on the pepper.

Leave, uncovered, in a cold place (refrigerator) for at least 3 hours.

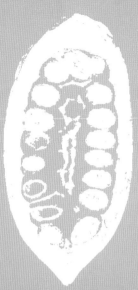

Ingredients

- 90g dark chocolate
- 1 pinch lemon pepper (can be found in specialist shops)

"When the great day arrived, Charlie ⊙
was always presented with one
small chocolate bar to eat all by himself."
(Roald Dahl, *Charlie and the Chocolate Factory*)

82 ◈ Dark chocolate with macadamia nuts and dried raspberries

Melt the dark chocolate using a bain-marie. Stir constantly until you have a smooth consistency, or temper the chocolate according to the method described on pages 11 and 12 (tempering).

Add the nuts and raspberries and mix well.

Pour into a chocolate bar mould, evenly distributing the pieces of nut and the raspberries.

Smooth by gently shaking the mould from side to side.

Leave, uncovered, in a cold place (refrigerator) for at least 3 hours.

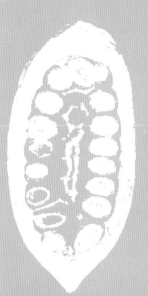

Ingredients

- 70g dark chocolate
- 10g macadamia nuts
- 10g dried raspberries

"Once you consume chocolate, chocolate will consume you."
(Anonymous)

84 ❖ Dark chocolate with glacé cherries

Melt the dark chocolate using a bain-marie. Stir constantly until you have a smooth consistency, or temper the chocolate according to the method described on pages 11 and 12 (tempering).

Pour into the chocolate bar mould.

Smooth by gently shaking the mould from side to side.

Arrange the cherries according to their colour and press them lightly into the chocolate.

Leave, uncovered, in a cold place (refrigerator) for at least 3 hours.

 Ingredients

- 80g dark chocolate
- 6 to 12 glacé cherries of different colours (about 35g depending on their size)

"If you've got melted chocolate all
over your hands, you're eating it too slowly."
(Anonymous)

85 ❖ Dark chocolate with poppy seeds

Melt the dark chocolate using a bain-marie. Stir constantly until you have a smooth consistency, or temper the chocolate according to the method described on pages 11 and 12 (tempering).

Add about half of the poppy seeds to the chocolate and mix well.

Pour the chocolate into a chocolate bar mould.

Smooth by gently shaking the mould from side to side.

Sprinkle the rest of the poppy seeds on top so as to cover the whole surface.

Leave, uncovered, in a cold place (refrigerator) for at least 3 hours.

Ingredients

- 90g dark chocolate
- 10g poppy seeds

"Eating chocolate can have significant influences on mood, generally leading to an increase in pleasant feelings and a reduction in tension." (Peter Rogers)

86 ❖ Dark chocolate with soft nougat

Cut out pieces of nougat exactly the same size as the squares of the chocolate bar mould and about half as thick as the height of the mould.

To make a chequered pattern you will need a number of squares of nougat equal to half the number of squares in your mould.

Arrange the pieces of nougat in the mould in a chequered pattern (by alternating an empty square and a square of nougat).

Dice the rest of the nougat into small cubes.

Melt the dark chocolate using a bain-marie. Stir constantly until you have a smooth consistency, or temper the chocolate according to the method described on pages 11 and 12 (tempering).

Add the cubes of nougat to the chocolate and mix well.

Pour the chocolate and cubes of nougat into the mould.

Smooth by gently shaking the mould from side to side.

Leave, uncovered, in a cold place (refrigerator) for at least 3 hours.

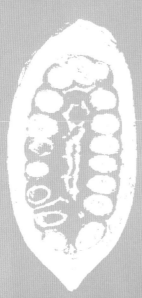

Ingredients

- 80g dark chocolate
- 15g soft nougat

88 ◈ Dark chocolate with almond paste

Melt the dark chocolate using a bain-marie. Stir constantly until you have a smooth consistency, or temper the chocolate according to the method described on pages 11 and 12 (tempering).

Pour half of the chocolate into the chocolate bar mould to make the first layer.

Cut out one, or several sheets of almond paste so that when put together they are exactly the size of the chocolate bar mould. They should be about 4mm thick. Place this layer of almond paste on top of the first layer of chocolate.

Pour on the rest of the chocolate, and smooth by gently shaking the mould from side to side.

Leave, uncovered, in a cold place (refrigerator) for at least 3 hours.

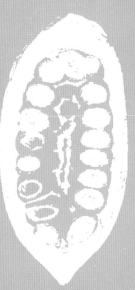

Ingredients

- 60g dark chocolate
- 30g almond paste (coloured or not)

"The superiority of chocolate, both for health and
nourishment, will soon give it the same preference
over tea and coffee in America which it has in Spain."
(Thomas Jefferson)

90 ❖ Dark chocolate with aniseed

Melt the dark chocolate using a bain-marie. Stir constantly until
you have a smooth consistency, or temper the chocolate according
to the method described on pages 11 and 12 (tempering).

Add about three quarters of the aniseed to the chocolate and mix
well.

Pour the chocolate into a chocolate bar mould.

Smooth by gently shaking the mould from side to side.

Sprinkle the rest of the aniseed on top.

Leave, uncovered, in a cold place (refrigerator) for at least 3 hours.

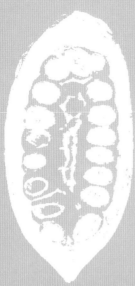

Ingredients

- 90g dark chocolate
- 2 dessertspoons dried green aniseed

"What you see before you, my friend, is the result of a lifetime of chocolate. A pound a day often."
(Katharine Hepburn)

92 ❖ Dark chocolate with Madagascar vanilla

Slit the vanilla pod open along one side with a sharp knife. Use the knife blade to scrape out the inside and collect the seeds.

Melt the dark chocolate using a bain-marie with the vanilla pod. Stir constantly until you have a smooth consistency, or temper the chocolate according to the method described on pages 11 and 12 (tempering).

When the chocolate has reached the right temperature, remove the vanilla pod, add the vanilla seeds and mix well.

Pour the chocolate into a chocolate bar mould.

Smooth by gently shaking the mould from side to side.

Leave, uncovered, in a cold place (refrigerator) for at least 3 hours.

Alternative presentation:

Pour the chocolate into long ice cube moulds.

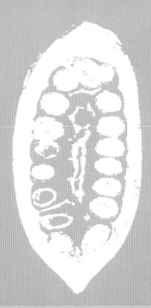

Ingredients

- 90g dark chocolate
- 1 pod Madagascar vanilla*

*Choose a good quality vanilla, such as the vanilla found in Madagascar. Quality pods can be recognised by the fact that they are pliable, with a granular appearance when you gently press the pod, and of course by their perfume.

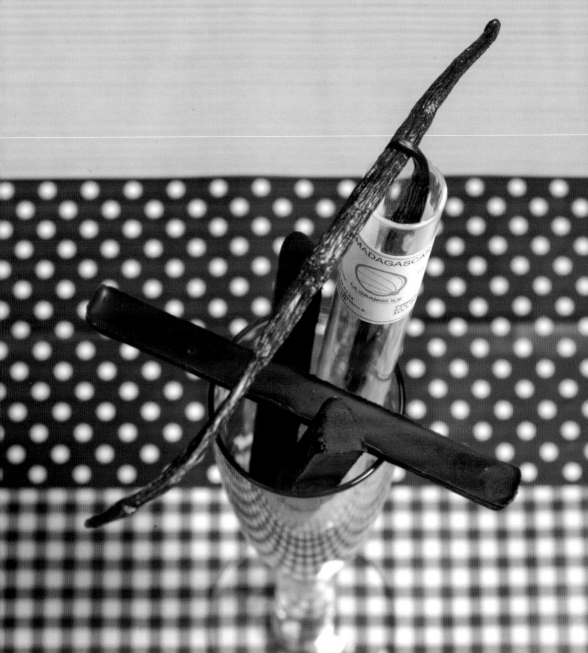

"Eat a chocolate bar before each meal. ⦾
It'll take the edge off your appetite."
(Anonymous)

94 ❖ Dark chocolate with cinnamon

Melt the dark chocolate using a bain-marie. Stir constantly until you have a smooth consistency, or temper the chocolate according to the method described on pages 11 and 12 (tempering).

Add half of the cinnamon (ie 1 dessertspoon) and mix well.

Pour the chocolate into a chocolate bar mould.

Smooth by gently shaking the mould from side to side.

Cool at room temperature for 15 minutes.

Sprinkle the rest of the cinnamon on top.

Leave, uncovered, in a cold place (refrigerator) for at least 3 hours.

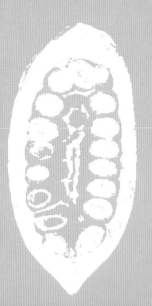

Ingredients

- 90g dark chocolate
- 2 dessertspoons powdered cinnamon

Acknowledgements

Thanks are due to Laurence Alemanno who has enlightened us on the subject of the origins of cocoa. After 14 years of research into the biology of the cacao tree, Laurence founded Chocolatitudes in Paris. Her boutique is devoted to organic chocolate. She organises workshops and talks on her favourite subject: chocolate!

Chocolatitudes
57 rue Daguerre
75014 Paris
tel: 01.42.18.49.02
www.chocolatitudes.com

This edition published 2010 by Waverley Books,
144 Port Dundas Road, Glasgow, G4 0HZ, Scotland

First published in France by Romain Pages Éditions 2009

English translation by Diana Sarran

ISBN 978 1 84934 040 3

A catalogue record for this book is available from the British Library.

Printed and bound in Indonesia